GOD
IS ON
YOUR SIDE
PARTICIPANT'S GUIDE

GOD
IS ON
YOUR SIDE

PARTICIPANT'S GUIDE

HOW JESUS IS FOR YOU WHEN EVERYTHING
SEEMS AGAINST YOU

Joshua Ryan Butler

MULTNOMAH

Multnomah

An imprint of the Penguin Random House Christian Publishing Group,
a division of Penguin Random House LLC

1745 Broadway, New York, NY 10019

waterbrookmultnomah.com
penguinrandomhouse.com

A Multnomah Trade Paperback Original

Portions of this work originally appeared in *God Is on Your Side*, copyright © 2025
by Joshua Ryan Butler, published in the United States by Multnomah,
an imprint of the Penguin Random House Christian Publishing
Group, a division of Penguin Random House LLC, in 2025.

Trade Paperback ISBN 978-0-593-44509-9
Ebook ISBN 978-0-593-44510-5

Printed in the United States of America on acid-free paper

1st Printing

The authorized representative in the EU for product safety and compliance is
Penguin Random House Ireland, Morrison Chambers, 32 Nassau Street,
Dublin D02 YH68, Ireland. https://eu-contact.penguin.ie

BOOK TEAM: Production editor: Laura Wright • Managing editor: Julia Wallace •
Production manager: Katie Zilberman • Copy editor: Kayla Fenstermaker •
Proofreaders: Sarah Kovac, Lisa Grimenstein

Book design by Caroline Cunningham
Title and part title page starburst: iiierlok_xolms/Adobe Stock

For details on special quantity discounts for bulk purchases,
contact specialmarketscms@penguinrandomhouse.com.

CONTENTS

SESSION III

SESSION IV

SESSION V

SESSION VI

SESSION VII

HOW TO USE THIS GUIDE

This study guide is designed to help you dive more deeply into the concepts at the heart of *God Is on Your Side:* to reflect on them and make them your own, to creatively explore their significance from fresh angles, to discuss those concepts with others or journal on their implications for your life, and to integrate and apply God's heart and vision for you.

This guide can be used individually or as part of a larger group (for example, a book club, a discussion gathering, or another kind of small group). Either way, you may want to grab some paper or a journal to record your thoughts as you work through the sessions. When you use this guide alongside the book, it will help you get as much out of the content as possible.

SESSION FORMAT

This guide is divided into seven sessions, with sessions typically covering two chapters (called mini-sessions) from

God Is on Your Side. Each mini-session contains four key components: Prepare Your Heart, Unpack It, Use Your Imagination, and Reflect on It. More on these components below.

Although this guide is structured to have seven sessions, go at your own pace. If you're reading the book in a group setting, then it might work best as a seven-week study with participants reading and reflecting on two chapters each week. Or your group may decide to stretch it out to a fourteen-week study. Do what works best for your schedule and timeline.

READING SCHEDULE

If you haven't already read the book *God Is on Your Side,* do so as you work your way through these sessions:

Session 1   Introduction and Chapter 1

Session 2   Chapters 2–3

Session 3   Chapters 4–5

Session 4   Chapters 6–7

Session 5   Chapters 8–9

Session 6   Chapters 10–11

Session 7   Chapters 12–13 and Conclusion

To follow is a summary of the four components you'll find in each mini-session.

1. Prepare Your Heart

This section will help you prepare your heart for the theme of the chapter. Use this space to reflect on an experience from your life that this chapter addresses.

2. Unpack It

Here you'll encounter questions designed to help you recap, unpack, and cement key insights from each chapter. Consider completing this section immediately after reading the chapter to record important takeaways and make them your own so you can return to them later for easy reference.

3. Use Your Imagination

These creative exercises are designed to help you reflect, using your imagination in unexpected ways, on a big idea from the chapter. These work best when you don't rush through them, so set aside ten to fifteen minutes, ideally, for each exercise. Allow your imagination to explore the exercise, and journal your reflections.

4. Reflect on It

These questions are intended to guide you in group discussion (or they can be used as journal prompts for personal reflection) about the significance of the chapter's central ideas for your own life and what it might look like to live out the big, beautiful realities you're exploring in the book.

As you walk through these discussion questions, you'll notice that I often ask multiple questions on the same topic—or I ask you something similar to help you go deeper in reflection or discussion with others. Don't worry about answering all of them (unless you want to). Feel free to home in on those that stand out to you.

GROUP LEADERS

If you're completing this study in a group setting and you're the facilitator of your group, here are some simple guidelines that can help make this seven-session journey more rewarding. Each session has enough content for sixty to ninety minutes of group time, depending on how long you desire to spend discussing each topic.

If you're part of an established small group going through *God Is on Your Side,* your group is probably familiar with how to review content in studies similar to this one. It may not be necessary to prescribe every detail of the meetings, though this brief refresher may help you prepare for the discussion.

Read and Pray

Before meeting with the group, read the chapters of *God Is on Your Side* associated with the upcoming session (see the reading schedule on page x) and complete the mini-sessions. Then pray for each person in your group and for your upcoming time together.

Group Members

Encourage every group member to read the assigned chapters of *God Is on Your Side* and complete the mini-sessions before they arrive at each meeting.

Getting Started

Once your group members have arrived, settle into a place free of distractions, where you can sit comfortably for the next hour or so. Then, when you're ready to get started, ask a group member to read the questions, one at a time, from the Reflect on It section. Encourage discussion of these questions and remember to take your time. (You can also allow participants to share reflections that stood out to them from the Unpack It and Use Your Imagination sections, depending on how much time you have and how many people are in your group.)

As you lead your group through this guide, keep these pro tips in mind:

- *Make time for each person to share.* The goal is to get everyone talking so every voice is heard and included in the discussion. This doesn't mean everybody needs to share on each question, but be mindful of a few people dominating the discussion.
- *Don't make everyone share.* This book gets into some sensitive topics. Some people might not be comfortable sharing their thoughts or experiences, or they might be in process and not ready to share yet. Respect that. Don't pressure people to contribute who aren't ready or don't want to.

· · ·

My hope is, by the end of the book and this guide, you'll have a bigger, more captivating vision of God and how he wants to encounter you in your life. I know I've been affected tremendously by reflecting on the concepts at the heart of the book. I hope you are too.

In Christ,
Josh

SESSION I

INTRODUCTION

On Your Side

Is God on my side? Is he really for me? It's easy to answer "Yes!" when life is going well. When your body's healthy, your bank account's full, and your best friends are by your side. It's harder to believe when life takes a turn for the worse. In the wake of disappointment and loss, you can find yourself wondering, *Is my maker for me? Does my savior have my back? Is God committed to my good?*

Where do you go when you wrestle with such questions?

PREPARE YOUR HEART

What drew you to pick up this book? Is there a question, circumstance, or need in your life that you're hoping the pages ahead will address?

Describe a season of life when you found it difficult to believe God was on your side. Perhaps it was a season of loss, hurt or betrayal in a relationship, an unexpected health condition, fear for your financial future, or questions about faith. Perhaps it was something else. Perhaps you're in that season today. In your response, focus on how your view of God was affected by this experience—how your convictions deepened or changed and so on.

When I say God is on your side, do you have any suspicions, questions, or concerns? That's okay! List those here. Later you can return and see if they are adequately addressed as you work through the book.

UNPACK IT

In It with You, Fighting for You, Working Through You
In John 1, how do each of these three key images speak to God being on your side?

- the Word made flesh
- the Lamb of God
- the ladder with angels

On God's Side
God being on your side doesn't mean he *picks* sides.

- What did the angelic commander of God's armies tell Joshua in Joshua 5? How is this a good corrective to those who try to make it seem like God *takes* sides?
- Jesus came "full of grace and truth" (John 1:14). Why are both of these important in understanding his posture toward us?

- In what contexts might people say "God is on my side" when it isn't true to reality?

USE YOUR IMAGINATION

Just as people sat across from artist Marina Abramović and were moved by the experience of seeing and being seen, imagine yourself sitting across from Christ. Ask the Holy Spirit to open the eyes of your heart to encounter Christ. Close your eyes and contemplate his heart toward you. What parts of your story do you hope he sees? What aspects of his heart do you long to know more fully? Take some time with this; then jot down any observations you want to remember.

Why do you think it's so powerful to be seen by someone—not just looked at, but truly seen? What might this suggest about our deepest longings and the experience we were made for with God?

How might this frame a reason to read Scripture and pray—not to try to perform for God and earn his affection, but rather to encounter the God who pursues us in Christ, who is on our side, who sees us, knows us, and desires to transform us into his image?

REFLECT ON IT

1. Regarding the first question of this introduction—the thing that drew you to pick up this book—elaborate on how you're hoping the pages ahead will help.

2. To the extent you're comfortable, describe a season of life when you found it difficult to believe God was on your side. Perhaps it was a season of loss, hurt or betrayal in a relationship, an unexpected health condition, fear for your financial future, or questions about faith. What was your perception of God like in that experience?

3. Which of these three images stands out most to you? Why?

    a. the Word made flesh (*the Creator entering our side of creation*)

    b. the Lamb of God (*the Innocent One stepping onto our side on the cross*)

    c. the ladder with angels (*the Risen One bringing heaven to our side of earth*)

4. Which message do you most need to hear today: that God is in it with you, that he fights for you, or that he wants to work through you? Why? Describe what it might look like to live into this reality more fully.

5. Close with a prayer giving Christ thanks for his incarnation, crucifixion, resurrection, and ascension; for specific ways he's worked in the story of your life; and for his heart toward you in being on your side.

1

SET THE GPS

When You Don't Know Where You're Going

What do you do when you're not sure where you're going? When life's direction doesn't seem clear anymore? Jesus invites you to realign your GPS with his. In John 2, he shows us where his ministry is heading. It's a famous story, where Jesus turns water to wine at a wedding. At face value, we might misunderstand this as simply a display of his power. (*Cool party trick, Jesus!*) Yet Jesus is doing something much more here.

Jesus is giving us a sign of where his ministry is headed, a glimpse of the destination he's driving us toward. So buckle up; there's a journey ahead. Jesus is taking us to a resurrection wedding—where the rivers run with wine, the celebration never ends, and we encounter our destiny in union with God.

PREPARE YOUR HEART

Describe a time when you felt disoriented or without hope. What were the circumstances? What emotions did you experience? How long did it last? What was your perception of God in that season?

UNPACK IT

Resurrection Wedding

"On the third day," John tells us, "a wedding took place at Cana" (John 2:1). John uses time stamps like this to frame the stories that follow.

- What event does "the third day" foreshadow in John's gospel?
- How does a third-day wedding foreshadow what Jesus has come to accomplish?
- What does this first sign in John's gospel tell us about the destination Jesus has come to take us to?

When You've Run Out

- What social significance did running out of wine have for a family hosting a wedding in that day?
- "My hour has not yet come," Jesus tells his mother (John 2:4). What does "my hour" refer to in John's gospel?
- When Jesus turns water to wine, how does this foreshadow what he will accomplish at the cross?

Rivers of Wine

- Jesus makes *a lot* of wine—roughly 750 bottles. Imagine you're a guest at this wedding, where the party's already been going on for days, when this abundance of top-quality wine gets unexpectedly rolled out. What are you thinking and feeling? Describe your experience.

- Jesus's miracle has an Old Testament backdrop. The prophets said the Messiah would bring a wedding feast where the mountains would drip with wine (Isaiah 25:6–9; Joel 3:18; Amos 9:13–14). What might this suggest about why Jesus makes so much wine?

- Why does Jesus make this the first sign of his ministry?

- Beyond wine, what picture do the passages above paint of the future God wants to establish for us as his people?

The Seventh Vessel

- The six stone water jars, John tells us, were "for the Jewish rites of purification" (John 2:6, ESV). Jesus is intentional with the details he chooses for this miracle. What did these rites involve, and what was their purpose?

- How does Jesus's death on the cross fulfill this aspect of the sign?

- Why might John—who loved symbolism—highlight that there were *six* stone water jars?

Best for Last

- The climax of Jesus's first sign is a powerful picture of the gospel. In this living parable, who does the master of the banquet represent?
- Who is the Bridegroom in the gospel?
- In John's gospel, how has the best wine been saved for last?
- In the gospel, how is God like the master of the banquet delighting in the best wine poured out by the Bridegroom for his wedding with us as the bride?

USE YOUR IMAGINATION

A little secret: God turns water into wine all the time. Rain falls to the earth, soaks into the soil, and is absorbed by the vine. It eventually emerges in the grapes, which come bursting off the branches. With this miracle, Jesus is not contradicting nature but rather speeding up the process, through *himself* as the vine. Yet there's one more crucial step in the process of making wine: You have to crush the grapes.

Your imagination is powerful. Something happens when you don't stop at simply reading the details of a story but access your creativity to soak in the message more deeply. Draw a picture of each of the following parts of the process described above. It can be a simple picture, but allow your imagination to envision each stage of the process with all the vitality and color of God's creation.

- rain falling from the sky and soaking into the ground
- a vine's roots absorbing the water from the soil

- the water traveling through the vine's branches into the grapes
- the grapes being plucked off the branches by the gardener
- the grapes being crushed in the winepress and the juice flowing
- the wine being poured into a cup, ready to be savored

God designed creation to point to Jesus, who was crushed to bring forth resurrection wine. Reflect on the significance of Jesus's sacrifice for you. Write a prayer of gratitude. Try to be specific with aspects of your life that have been transformed by his sacrificial love, his cleansing, and his heart of abundance toward you.

REFLECT ON IT

1. Is there a time when you felt disoriented? Perhaps an unexpected event in your life left you feeling hopeless. To the extent you feel comfortable, summarize what happened. (Be brief so there's time for everyone to share.)

2. Jesus's miracle at Cana is the first sign of John's gospel, where Jesus sets the GPS to show us the destination his ministry is headed toward. How can reorienting our GPS toward our future in God's resurrection wedding bring hope when we feel hopeless?

3. The wedding runs out of wine, an embarrassing disaster for the host family. Have you ever had a time when you felt like you ran out, unable to meet people's ex-

pectations and disheartened with nothing left to give?
Describe what the experience was like.

4. Jesus makes *a lot* of wine (around 750 bottles)! Read
   Amos 9:13–14. How does the abundant kingdom Jesus
   has brought confront popular misconceptions people
   in our culture might have about God?

5. Jesus uses water jars from "the Jewish rites of purification" (John 2:6, ESV). This points to the purifying nature of his death (John 19:34). Describe how you feel
   when you emerge from a long hot shower or bath.
   Focus not just on your external state but on how you
   feel on the inside. How might this compare to the
   cleansing Jesus came to bring?

6. Do you ever struggle with feeling dirty, stained, or
   guilty? Where in your life do these feelings show up?
   Do they make you feel distant from God or unworthy
   of his love? Consider expressing this to God, either
   through writing it out in a prayer or through sharing it
   with the group. Reflect together on the immensity of
   Christ's love for you—that he would shed his blood to
   cover you and wash you spotlessly clean—and what
   this does to stir your affections for God.

7. You're invited not simply to attend God's resurrection
   wedding but to be the bride. What kind of depth of
   union and vitality of celebration does this imply you
   were created to experience with God? What might it
   look like to begin preparing for this future and living
   toward this reality today?

8. Close with prayer, asking God to "set your GPS" and
   orient your life toward this destination.

SESSION II

2

BRING DOWN THE HOUSE

When Change Is Painful

What do you do when change is painful? When Jesus shows up with confrontation rather than comfort, turning your life upside down? When the place where you once encountered God now seems to be crumbling around you? It can be easy to think God is against you, but what if this is part of his being more deeply on your side? What if he goes all bull-in-a-china-shop because he's willing to crash through your distance and crush your idols to get to your heart?

PREPARE YOUR HEART

Describe a time when change in your life was painful. Perhaps Jesus confronted a pattern of sin in your life or convicted you of something you needed to address and apologize for. Or perhaps things you'd relied on came crumbling down around you; a job or relationship you'd thought was stable ended up being precarious. What were the circumstances?

What emotions did you experience? How long did the season last? What was your perception of God in that season?

UNPACK IT

Demolition God

- What Old Testament story did the Passover festival celebrate?
- What animal from Passover is Jesus described as in John's gospel? (See John 1:29, 36.)
- At the climax of John's gospel, Jesus goes up to Jerusalem to be crucified during Passover. What does this suggest about how the temple scene in John 2 and the Crucifixion are connected?
- Many people assume Jesus turns over tables and drives people out of the temple because he's angry with folks selling stuff there. (*Get that bookstore out of the church lobby!*) Why is this an insufficient answer? (*Hint:* Read Deuteronomy 14:24–26.)
- What three examples does this chapter of *God Is on Your Side* give of Old Testament prophets doing symbolic acts?
- What symbolic meaning does this suggest for Jesus's disruptive actions in the temple?
- List two details from John 2 that show Jesus is not losing his cool but doing something deliberate and premeditated.

Divine Renovation

- Read Jeremiah 7:9–11 for a clue as to why the old temple would one day need to be demolished. What practices that God was confronting stand out to you?
- Compare Jeremiah's list to the Ten Commandments (Deuteronomy 5:6–21). How many commands were being broken?
- Why is it a problem that they were hiding out in the temple while continuing to do all these things?
- What do you think God meant by saying his house had become "a den of robbers" (Jeremiah 7:11)?

The Crucifixion as Demolition

Jesus's dramatic performance in the temple is a sign of his own coming crucifixion, where he will be torn down as the true temple. Describe how these details from John 2 foreshadow the cross:

- cracking the whip
- driving out the sacrificial animals
- turning over the tables
- driving out the people
- pouring out the coins

USE YOUR IMAGINATION

Imagine Jesus's crucifixion as the destruction of a temple. Draw the following images: a sledgehammer, embroidered curtains, coins poured out, a table overturned, a lamb driven away, a cloud, and brick rubble. As you draw each image, reflect on the aspect of Christ's death it speaks to: a sledgehammer (the whipping of his body), curtains (the stripping of his clothes), coins (the cost he paid for sin), a table (his body overturned upon the cross), a lamb (the sacrificial animals that would no longer be needed), a cloud (the glory departing the temple of his body as Jesus exhaled his final breath), and rubble (the burial of his remains). It's okay if you're not a great artist; feel free to keep the images simple. The point is more to spark your imagination to reflect on the power of Christ's death.

Close with a prayer of thanks to Jesus for his sacrifice, his willingness to be torn down for you so that you might be rebuilt in him.

Bonus: Consider listening to the worship song "Resurrender."[*] Reflect on your identity as a living temple (the lyrics of this song are powerfully centered on this theme). What area of your life might Jesus be calling you to resurrender in obedience to him?

REFLECT ON IT

1. Is there a time when Jesus confronted sin in your life or when things you'd relied on came crumbling down around you? Describe the experience. Was the change painful? Where did you find the motivation to do the difficult thing or the strength to endure the aftermath?

[*] Track 3 on *Team Night (Live)*, Hillsong Worship, Hillsong Music and Resources LLC, 2022.

2. Read John 2:14–15. Have you ever wrestled with understanding why Jesus turned over tables and drove people out of the temple? What insights from this chapter of *God Is on Your Side* stood out to you to help make sense of this scene?

3. Sometimes people call this event the cleansing of the temple, but Jesus isn't cleaning up the temple—he's symbolically tearing it down. Why do you think God cares so much about the purity of his people? What does it do in your heart to know he's committed to building you up on a firm foundation, even when such change is painful?

4. In Jeremiah 7:9–11, God confronted people hiding in the temple when they weren't living according to his ways. Describe some contemporary ways we hide in church while living far from God. What circumstances have you seen in your life or the lives of people you know? Or what broader themes have you observed in the church at large?

5. This chapter describes the death of Jesus as the tearing down of the true temple. Talk about Jesus's crucifixion as a temple being torn down. What details stand out to you? How do images from this scene in John 2 foreshadow the cross?

6. We get to "bring down the house" in worship of Christ, our king, in response to all that he's done for us. How is worship as a response to what Christ has done for you more powerful than trying to use worship to get him on your side? In what ways are you inspired to worship Christ more fully—whether in the

weekly gathering with your church or in all of your life—in light of his great love for you?

7. Jesus wants to make you a living temple. In what areas of your life do you sense him calling you to a deeper level of obedience? Feel free to share these with the group and then pray for one another along these lines.

3

BECOME THE BELOVED

When You Don't Feel Wanted

Where do you go when you feel unwanted? Maybe you look for affection in the arms of another. Maybe you lower your standards and settle for someone who treats you like dirt. Maybe you self-harm to feel something again or rely on substances to numb the pain. Maybe you isolate, protecting your heart by locking it in a cage where no one can hurt you again. If you feel rejected, dropped, or discarded, there's good news: Jesus is on his way.

PREPARE YOUR HEART

Think of a time when you felt unwanted. Perhaps you experienced rejection in relationships, the disappointment of unrequited affection, or the solitary confinement of being alone. Perhaps this is even a season you're currently in. Describe the season. What were the circumstances? What emotions did you experience? How long did it last? What was your perception of God in that season?

UNPACK IT

First Encounter

On his way through Samaria, "Jesus, tired as he was from the journey, sat down by [Jacob's] well" (John 4:6). The well might seem like a passing detail, but it echoes significant scenes in the Old Testament. Read the following passages and jot down which brides were first met at a well, as well as any details you see echoed in John 4:

- Genesis 24:12–19
- Genesis 29:1–14
- Exodus 2:15–21

The renowned Jewish scholar Robert Alter described the well as a betrothal type-scene, common in ancient Hebrew literature, with the following five elements. Skim through John 4 and write down which verses correspond to these elements:

1. The future groom journeys to a foreign land.
2. There he encounters a girl at a well.
3. One of them draws water from the well. (*Note:* Pay attention to the discussion of living water, who will give it, and what that water symbolizes.)
4. The girl rushes home with news of the stranger's arrival.
5. A betrothal is concluded after he has been invited to a meal.[*] (*Note:* There isn't a literal betrothal in the John

---

[*] Robert Alter, *The Art of Biblical Narrative*, rev. ed. (Basic Books, 2011), 62. A representative can stand in for the future groom, as in Genesis 24, where Abraham's servant discovered Rebekah for Isaac.

passage, since Jesus's encounter with the Samaritan woman is platonic, yet look for which verses echo this element.)

Boundary Crosser

- Why did Jews and Samaritans avoid each other?
- If Jesus doesn't *have* to go through Samaria for geographical reasons, why does John tell us he "had to" go there (John 4:4)? What drives him there?

Thirst Quencher

- Jesus offers the woman "living water" (John 4:10). What kind of water sources did *living water* refer to in the ancient world?
- Why were such water sources vital to ancient peoples? What benefits did they bring?
- How does living water represent the work of the Holy Spirit in our lives?
- Why is it significant that Jesus is the one who gives this Holy Spirit to his bride?

Five Husbands

- While it might be easy today to assume this woman had five husbands because of her own immorality, why is it more likely that she had been rejected and mistreated by men?
- From another angle, however, the Samaritan woman also likely represents the checkered past of her people. Describe the Old Testament backdrop that suggests the symbolic significance of the five husbands.

Tell the Town

The Samaritan woman runs back to tell the whole town about Jesus.

- How does the Samaritan woman's response speak to the evangelistic calling of the church?
- How do the Samaritans respond when they encounter Jesus?

USE YOUR IMAGINATION

Jesus is the boundary-crossing, thirst-quenching, stone-rolling seventh husband! He is the One your heart was made for. Where did you first meet him? Reflect on that season of your life and how you came to know him. Invite the Holy Spirit to guide your memory back to key moments and details from your story. Draw images that represent that season. For example,

- If you were addicted, you might draw a symbol of what you were addicted to.
- If you were lonely, you might draw a symbol of your emotional state at that time.
- If Christ brought peace, you might draw a picture of a dove.

The point here is not to draw the "right" picture perfectly but to catalyze your imagination with symbols that represent where Christ met you, what that encounter was like, and the impact it made on your life. If you don't like drawing, consider narrating the story of your first encounter with Christ.

You can use these symbols in the future. When you feel haunted by your past, when you're worried about being unwanted, when you experience fear in your relationship with God, go back to the well—back to that place where you first met, where you encountered Christ's love for you and heard him call you his own. Tell your testimony—not just to the town, but to yourself. Recount his covenantal love for you. Preach the gospel to your heart. Let his commitment to you refresh your heart.

REFLECT ON IT

1. What are your favorite first-encounter scenes? This could be a scene from a movie or another piece of pop culture. Or if you're married, it could be the moment when you first met your spouse. Or it could be a funny or romantic story from a couple you know.

2. Jesus "sat down by the well" (John 4:6). What stood out to you the most from this chapter's discussion of the biblical motif of the well as the location where a groom first meets his bride? Why is it significant to remember where we first encountered Jesus and how he captivated our hearts?

3. Jews and Samaritans hated one another for religious, political, and cultural reasons. What types of people are you tempted to write off today or distance yourself from, rather than pursue with the love of Jesus? Within the church, what unnecessary dividing lines do you see fracturing the bride Jesus came to unite? (That's not to say we shouldn't have convictions or healthy

boundaries, but focus on any unnecessary dividing lines of hostility that stand out to you.)

4. Jesus crosses multiple boundaries to get to the woman at the well. What cultural divides or lines of hostility might he be challenging you to cross in order to pursue people around you?

5. What boundaries did Jesus cross to get to your heart? What unlikely places did he enter in your life to make you his own? How can remembering this aspect of your story remind you how much you are wanted by God as his beloved?

6. Jesus offers living water. What popular substitutes does our culture offer to try to quench our thirst for meaning and significance? Why do you think Jesus is able to quench our thirst in ways far beyond any of the substitutes out there?

7. Unlike Nicodemus, who approached Jesus at night, the Samaritan woman encounters him in the light of day. While Nicodemus represented the old temple, the Samaritan woman foreshadows the church as a new and living temple. How can encountering Christ vulnerably "in the light," rather than hiding "in the dark," make you a living temple for his presence? Have you experienced this in your own life?

8. The Samaritan woman runs excitedly to tell the whole town about Jesus. What did you think of this chapter's suggestion that sharing what Jesus has done in your life should be similar to announcing an engagement? How might it change evangelism to approach it less like a chess match and more like setting someone up on a blind date with the person you think is best for them?

9. Where did you first meet Christ? How did you encounter him? What season of life were you in? There will likely not be time for everyone to share their fuller story, so aim for a simple thirty-second to one-minute summary that gives a few key details, such as (1) where you lived, (2) how old you were, and (3) what about Jesus drew you to him. If you aren't yet a Christian, you might simply share something you find interesting or compelling about Jesus currently. (*Note:* For the sake of time, it could be helpful for the group leader to use a one-minute timer to keep members on track so that everyone gets to share.) After everyone shares, take time to pray and celebrate the work of Christ in one another's lives.

SESSION III

4

ENDURE THE HARDEST MILES

When Jesus Answers Only Half Your Prayer

The hardest part of a marathon is the last six miles. Your energy runs out and you hit the wall. This is where you begin to think, *I've got nothing left; I can't do this* (even though your body actually can). The battle is more mental than physical. The hardest part is the battle within.

Maybe you're in the last six miles of a marathon right now. A long-lasting season of difficulty, loss, or fear. There's hope, friend. Let's lace up and learn how to lean in when we're lagging, how to press forward and trust Jesus in our hardest miles, when it feels like we've got nothing left.

PREPARE YOUR HEART

Have you ever faced a marathon season—where you found yourself physically depleted, emotionally exhausted, and mentally worn thin? Describe that season, whether past or present. What were the circumstances? What emotions did you experience? How long did the season last? What was your perception of God during that time?

UNPACK IT

Half the Answer

- John 4 refers to *the third day* ("after the two days") and *Cana* ("where [Jesus] had turned the water into wine"), similar to the third-day miracle at the wedding in Cana (John 2). Why do you think John highlights details that echo this earlier story?
- What event does this foreshadow that Jesus will accomplish on the third day?
- When the royal official begs Jesus to come and heal his son, why do you think Jesus refuses to go with him?
- Imagine Jesus had accompanied him on the long journey home. What difference might this have made in his confidence and hope while returning?

Building Trust

- Jesus's response to the official's request can seem a bit harsh: "Unless you people see signs and wonders . . . you will never believe" (John 4:48). But Jesus isn't rebuking a scared parent for seeking the well-being of their child. What evidence from the passage supports this?
- How is the official an exemplar of faith?
- What gospel theme related to outsiders and insiders does this official illustrate?

The Journey Home

- Jesus sends the official home with a promise: "'Go,' Jesus replied, 'your son will live.' The man took Jesus at his word and departed" (John 4:50). Imagine the official's long-distance journey back home. What fears do you think he faced while walking toward the horizon?

The Finish Line

At the finish line, the official finds Jesus has been faithful: "While [the official] was still on the way, his servants met him with the news that his boy was living" (John 4:51).

- Imagine the scene. What might this father's reunion with his son have looked like?
- The official discovers his son was healed at "the exact time" Jesus spoke (verse 53). What does this say about the power of Jesus's word?

A Greater Prophet

"A prophet has no honor in his own hometown," John says to open the story (John 4:44, ESV). Like many prophets of old, Jesus is rejected on his home turf. Like the great prophets Elijah and Elisha, he raises a dying son. This Old Testament backdrop also provides a significant contrast with Jesus's actions here. Read 2 Kings 4:8–37 and answer the following questions:

- How did the Shunammite woman welcome the prophet Elisha?

- Did the woman accept Elisha's plan to not accompany her home (verses 29–30)? What might this suggest about the faith of the royal official in John 4?
- Did Elisha need to be physically present to heal her son (verse 31)? What might this suggest about the power of Jesus on display in John 4?
- Observe how Elisha accomplished the healing of the dead son (verses 32–35). Elijah used a similar method in 1 Kings 17:19–22. How does this foreshadow Christ's identification with us on the cross to raise us from the dead?

The Risen Son

Not only does Jesus raise the dying son; he is also the dying Son who is raised. John tells us this miracle is the second sign Jesus performs at Cana. This makes it a foreshadowing of the gospel, a picture of his death and resurrection.

- How is the royal official at the end of this miracle a picture of the Father?
- How is the royal son raised from the power of death a picture of Jesus?
- How are the royal servants who announce the good news a picture of the disciples?

USE YOUR IMAGINATION

The royal official traveled more than the length of a marathon to see Jesus and return back home. Close your eyes and try to imagine each of the three stages of his journey:

1. The journey to Jesus
2. The journey back home
3. Crossing the finish line

Jot down words or phrases that describe the different emotions you imagine he felt during each of these stages.

Think about the following parallels for your own life:

1. *The journey to Jesus.* How can this be a picture of contending in prayer? Is there a raw or difficult area of your life where you want to make time to proactively seek his presence and power?
2. *The journey back home.* How can this be a picture of trust? Is there an area where you haven't yet seen Christ answer your prayers and you feel him calling you to move from "what if" to "even if"?
3. *Crossing the finish line.* How can this be a picture of hope? How do you envision the coming resurrection meeting that area of painful need in your life? What would it look like to take Christ at his word and grow in trust today as you move toward that destination?

REFLECT ON IT

1. Have you ever been in a marathon season where you found yourself physically depleted, emotionally exhausted, and mentally worn thin? Briefly describe that season.
2. Jesus answers only half the royal official's prayer. Have

you ever had a season where Jesus answered only half your prayer? How did he use that season to build your trust?

3. What is the difference between "what if" and "even if"? Describe a season where Christ called you to move from "what if" to "even if."

4. Is there an area of your life where God is calling you to that shift today? Why is that shift hard? What powerful changes can it make in your outlook and experience?

5. The royal official "took Jesus at his word and departed" (John 4:50). What emotions do you imagine he experienced on that long journey home? Do you tend to view trust in Jesus as the absence of fear or as something you exercise in the midst of your fear? What difference does this make?

6. At the finish line, the official finds that Jesus has been faithful. How is this a picture of our coming resurrection? What do you think of this chapter's claim that, in light of the resurrection, the question is not *if* God will heal but *when*?

7. How does the coming healing of the resurrection confront the false teaching that God will always heal you *now* if only you have enough faith? How does Jesus's resurrection power confront the cynicism that says God *never* heals today, which can lead to passivity in prayer? In what areas is Christ inviting you to be more active in your prayer life? In what areas is Christ inviting you to trust him in the midst of yet-unanswered prayers?

8. Jesus's miracle here echoes the Old Testament stories of Elijah and Elisha, each a great prophet who raised

a dying son. Read aloud the following passage; then discuss how this is a picture of Christ's identification with us on the cross to raise us from the power of death.

> When Elisha reached the house, there was the boy lying dead on his couch. He went in, shut the door on the two of them and prayed to the LORD. Then he got on the bed and lay on the boy, mouth to mouth, eyes to eyes, hands to hands. As he stretched himself out on him, the boy's body grew warm. Elisha turned away and walked back and forth in the room and then got on the bed and stretched out on him once more. The boy sneezed seven times and opened his eyes. (2 Kings 4:32–35)

9. Per the earlier section, Jesus's raising of the dying son is a sign. Discuss how this miracle foreshadows Christ's death and resurrection. How is the royal official a picture of the Father? Who is a picture of Jesus? Who do the servants announcing the good news represent?

10. Close in prayer. Consider breaking into groups of two or three people to pray together for any areas where you need to either (1) *go to Jesus* and pray more boldly for healing or (2) *trust in Jesus* in the midst of an unanswered prayer.

5

RISE UP

When You're Stuck and Can't Get Out of Bed

What do you do when you're stuck and can't get out of bed? When you feel overwhelmed by a depression you can't lift, a dread you can't shake, a debt you can't pay? When someone asks, "Can I help you?" their tone matters. Depending on the inflection of someone's voice, those four simple words can communicate (1) a genuine offer of assistance, (2) annoyance at an intrusion, or (3) a plea for someone's best. Let's see how Jesus uses all three tones to ultimately extend a hand and offer a plea for our best.

PREPARE YOUR HEART

Reflect on a time when you desperately needed help. What were the circumstances? What emotions did you feel during that time? Were you surrounded by supportive community or isolated? Did anyone let you down? Did anyone rise to the occasion and help you? How did this season shape your sense of God's closeness or distance to you in times of need? Don't feel pressure to repeat the clichéd answers you know in your head to be true. Just name the reality of how the experience shaped you.

UNPACK IT

An Offer of Assistance
Jesus enters Jerusalem and goes to the Sheep Gate, where "a great number of disabled people used to lie" (John 5:3).

- Why do you think Jesus goes straight here to the "hospital," rather than to the healthy, upbeat places in the capital city? What does this suggest about his priorities?
- What does Jesus's identity as the Good Shepherd (John 10:11) mean for those who are his hurting sheep, such as those by the Sheep Gate here?
- Jesus asks the paralyzed man, "Do you want to get well?" (John 5:6). Why do you think Jesus asks him this?

Life Under the Law
- The man has been paralyzed for thirty-eight years. What other biblical story does this number show up in? (*Hint:* See Deuteronomy 2:14.) What is its significance there?
- How does the paralyzed man represent Israel's condition more broadly?
- What do the five porches represent in the early church's interpretation of this scene?

An Annoying Intrusion

- Jesus intentionally heals this man on the Sabbath, and because of this, "the Jewish leaders began to persecute him" (John 5:16). What rationale does Jesus give for his actions?

- Unique offices in Israel were exempt from certain Sabbath restrictions. What kind of authority do Jesus's actions here suggest he has over creation?

Practice Resurrection

- Jesus uses the raising of the paralyzed man as an illustration of the coming resurrection. How is this man on his mat a picture of our spiritual condition without Christ?

- Resurrection is good news, but what warning does Jesus give in John 5:28–29?

- How does this warning make sense of his saying, "Stop sinning or something worse may happen to you" (verse 14)?

- How is the pool of Bethesda in this passage a picture of baptism?

- How is this miracle a picture of Jesus's own death and resurrection?

USE YOUR IMAGINATION

It's easy to feel stuck under the weight of the law—unable to rise up out of bed—instead of living by grace. While we are no longer under the Old Testament law, we can still be tempted to think our belonging with God is based on our performance and ability to measure up to expectations, social codes, and rules of behavior.

Reflect on the following areas of life and write down the expectations you feel you've failed to measure up to (whether your own, God's, or someone else's) and the expectations you experience pressure to measure up to in order to be truly accepted:

- family (*parents, spouse, kids, singleness, etc.*)
- friends (*who you know*)
- appearance (*how you look*)
- work (*what you do*)
- online (*your social media presence*)
- money (*the lifestyle you can afford*)
- status (*how you're perceived*)

What would it look like to live by grace rather than law? Looking at the list above, take some time to prayerfully discern between these expectations:

1. Unhealthy expectations that aren't from God, which Christ wants to set you free from (draw an X through these)
2. Healthy expectations that would be good to grow in, while remembering that Christ wants to set you free from thinking your belonging is based on your performance rather than his grace (circle these)

Bring these areas to Christ in prayer. Place yourself in this scene from John 5, using the following movements:

- *Envision yourself on the mat; see him standing before you.* Take three deep breaths, slowly inhaling and exhaling, to center yourself in prayer leading into this.

- *Name the areas you feel stuck in; hear him ask, "Do you want to get well?"* Focus on the power of his word and on the authority of the One who stands before you.
- *Envision yourself taking up your mat to walk; thank him for his grace.* Pray into the truths about Jesus from this chapter, celebrating who he is and what his presence means in your life.

REFLECT ON IT

1. Have you ever had unexpected help in a time of desperate need? What was the situation? Who helped you? How was this a window into the nature of grace?

2. Jesus enters the "bright lights, big city" of Jerusalem and goes directly to the "hospital" with the disabled community. What does this suggest about his priorities? Do you tend to think he's more interested in your Jerusalem or your Sheep Gate—that is, your trophies or your scars?

3. Jesus's question "Do you want to get well?" gives the paralyzed man a voice. Why do you think it's important that people with disabilities—and others who tend to be excluded—are given a voice and agency in their family, church, and community? Why is it significant that Jesus calls you to be not just a *recipient* of his grace but a *participant* in his kingdom?

4. Read the William Barclay quote on page 78. The early church saw the paralyzed man as a representative for

Israel under the curse of the law. Describe in your own words the difference between living under law and living by grace.

5. In this chapter, I share from my own battle of learning to live by grace rather than under law (page 70). When have you struggled with this? When have you felt stuck in your failure to live up to expectations (whether your own, God's, or someone else's)? Or pressured to measure up in order to be accepted? What would living by grace look like in your own life?

6. Jesus defends his healing on the Sabbath not by denying that he's working but rather by pointing to his identity as the Son of the Father. Jesus has a 24-7 pass to all of creation. What areas of your life are you tempted to restrict him from having full access to? Why do you think you're afraid of submitting these areas to him? What would it look like to give him authority in these areas?

7. Jesus uses this miracle as a picture of the coming resurrection. How is being stuck on the mat a picture of our condition without Christ? While resurrection is good news, what warning does he give in verses 28–29? Why is Jesus's offer of assistance a plea for our best (the *third* tone from this chapter)?

8. What would it look like for you to practice resurrection? In what areas are you convicted to move away from the death-dealing ways of sin and live into the light of God's love? To prepare for the coming kingdom Christ will raise you into? Share these and then spend time praying for one another along these lines.

SESSION IV

6

FEAST IN THE WILDERNESS

When Your Soul Is Starving

W here do you go when your soul is starving? When you hunger for more than bread? When you crave meaning and connection and are famished for a revelation from God? Jesus wants to satisfy your deepest hunger. When Jesus feeds more than five thousand people with a few loaves and fish, this is just an appetizer: a picture of what he's come to bring *you* through his cross and resurrection.

PREPARE YOUR HEART

Describe a time when you felt a soul hunger, a craving for deeper meaning and purpose. What were the circumstances? Was there a backdrop of discouragement or disappointment? How did you try to cope with the craving? If there was an eventual resolution, what was it? How would you counsel yourself if you could go back and sit across the table from the person you were back then?

UNPACK IT

Better Bread

- When Jesus asks his disciples how they can feed the great crowd, Andrew emphasizes how little they have: "five small barley loaves and two small fish" (John 6:9). What do you think Jesus is trying to teach his disciples by asking them for a plan when he already knows what he's going to do?

- John highlights an important Old Testament back-drop to this scene: God feeding Israel manna in the wilderness. Read John 6:1–4. List three details that echo how Moses led Israel in the Old Testament.

- Jesus "made" the people "sit down" in a place with "plenty of grass" (John 6:10).* Compare Psalm 23:1–2. What do you think John is suggesting about Jesus in this scene?

- Everyone had "as much as they wanted," and the crowd "all had enough to eat" (John 6:11–12). Compare Exodus 16:21. What does this suggest about Jesus's ability to provide?

A Test in the Wilderness

When Jesus asks Philip for a plan, "he asked this only to test him, for he already had in mind what he was going to do" (John 6:6).

---

* "Made" is a more literal rendering of *poieō* than "had," which also makes the Psalm 23 echo clearer.

- In the Old Testament, the Lord tested his people in the wilderness "in order to know what was in [their] heart" (Deuteronomy 8:2). Similarly, here, why do you think Jesus wants to know what is in his people's heart?
- Twice in John 6, the crowds grumble against Jesus (verses 41, 61). How does this point back to Israel's wilderness wandering? (*Hint:* Compare Numbers 11:4–5.)

More Than Enough

Jesus performs this miracle with attention to detail; some of these details suggest a symbolic significance.

- What do the five loaves of bread symbolize?
- What do the twelve baskets of leftover bread symbolize?
- How did the law bring both a nourishing blessing and the weight of a curse?

Come Hungry

"I am the living bread that came down from heaven," Jesus explains. "This bread is my flesh, which I will give for the life of the world" (John 6:51).

- How does this fifth sign foreshadow Christ's crucifixion?
- Jesus says, *Eat my flesh; drink my blood* (verses 53–56). While the major church traditions approach the presence of Jesus in the Lord's Supper differently, what do the vast majority have in common?

Feast on Jesus

Jesus won't turn you away. "Whoever comes to me will never go hungry," he says. "Whoever comes to me I will never drive away" (John 6:35, 37).

- What are some of the main substitutes our culture promotes to satisfy our souls?
- How might Scripture, prayer, and other spiritual formation practices relate to feasting on food Jesus provides?

USE YOUR IMAGINATION

We need life from outside ourselves to survive. It's easy to forget this in our modern society, where food comes shrink-wrapped in the grocery store. We can miss the connection between the grains of wheat severed from the stalk and the slice of bread we pop into the toaster. Or the butchered beast, its life given to give us life, and the burger we order at the drive-through.

Think of three foods in a favorite meal (a protein, a carb, and a fruit or vegetable). Consider the various stages they go through from farm to table, and draw a picture representing each stage for each food. (It's okay if you're not a great visual artist; a basic picture is fine. The point is simply to catalyze your imagination.)

At what stage is life given (the fruit plucked, the stalk severed, and so on)? How might this speak to a cycle of giving and receiving embedded in creation? How might this point to Christ's greater sacrifice, his life given for us? What does this say about our dependency on life received from outside ourselves—both physically and spiritually—in order to truly live? What would a posture of dependence on and gratitude toward God look like in your life?

REFLECT ON IT

1. In this chapter, I describe a season of heartbreak that left me hungry for much more than food. Describe a time when you felt a hunger for deeper meaning and purpose. What were the circumstances? How did you try to cope with the craving? What brought eventual resolution, if there was one?

2. In John's gospel, Andrew emphasizes how little they have to feed the crowd, but Jesus can do a lot with our little. In what area of your life do you feel like you have only a little to face a big situation? What would it look like to trust Christ in this situation, focusing more on the *who* than the *how*? (If someone in the group is facing a major issue, take time to pray over them.)

3. Jesus is presented as a new and greater Moses in this chapter of *God Is on Your Side*. What details stood out to you that echo this background of Israel in the wilderness? In what ways does the church live in the wilderness today on our way to the promised land? What does it look like for us to rely on heavenly bread on this journey?

4. The crowds grumble against Jesus twice in this passage—like Israel grumbled against Moses in the wilderness. Have you ever grumbled against Jesus?

When he didn't meet your expectations? When your soul was starving and you weren't sure he cared to fill it? Describe a time when you succumbed to "smoldering discontent."[*] In what way were you tempted to go "back to Egypt"? Why do you think we're tempted to trade our freedom for bread?

5. Why is it significant that Jesus feeds his people more than enough, with leftovers to spare? Do you tend to think of him as generous or stingy when it comes to your physical needs? What about when it comes to your spiritual needs?

6. We need life from outside ourselves to survive. Jesus says he is "the living bread that came down from heaven" (John 6:51). How does our need for bread point to our greater need for Christ? How does this confront the myth in our culture that we can do life on our own?

7. Jesus says, *Eat my flesh; drink my blood.* The major church traditions see Jesus's real presence available to us in the Lord's Supper (though they have different ways of understanding *how* this happens). What is your own understanding or experience of the Lord's Supper? How might the Old Testament imagery of God providing heavenly bread for his people in the wilderness speak to this New Testament practice? How can you approach the Lord's Table with more intentionality or awe as a sacrament through which to encounter Christ?

8. When it comes to your deepest spiritual hunger, what substitutes are you most tempted by? Do you tend to

---

[*] "1111. Gogguzó," Bible Hub, accessed February 12, 2025, https://biblehub.com/greek/1111.htm.

approach Scripture, prayer, and spiritual formation practices as feasting or as rote activities to check off a list? How might approaching them as feasting change your mindset and experience?

9. What does it look like for you to feast on Christ in this season? After sharing, pray for one another along these lines.

7

BLOW THE DAM

When You're Suffering Divine Dehydration

Where do you go when you feel blocked from the life-giving presence of God? We were made for abundant life in the kingdom of God, but sin is an obstacle—like a dam—that has cut us off from the river of life. Jesus has come to blow the dam and bring us water in the wilderness.

PREPARE YOUR HEART

Reflect on a time when you felt distant from God's life-giving presence. What were the circumstances? How did you try to address it? What practices have you found helpful in such seasons? How would you counsel yourself if you could go back and sit across the table from yourself?

UNPACK IT

Bring Your Thirst

"On the last and greatest day of the festival," John tells us, "Jesus stood and said in a loud voice, 'Let anyone who is thirsty come to me and drink'" (John 7:37).

- What event in Israel's history did the Festival of Tabernacles commemorate?
- How did Israel celebrate the festival?
- How does this shed light on Jesus's theme of thirst?
- List a few ways clean water is foundational for life today.

All You Need Is Need

"Jesus stood up and cried out, 'If anyone thirsts, let him come to me and drink'" (John 7:37, ESV).

- Read Isaiah 55:1. How does this verse enrich your understanding of Jesus's invitation?
- Read Isaiah 55:2. What unsatisfying substitutes does our culture tempt people to "spend" themselves on?
- The term "cried out" (*krazō*) comes from the sound of a raven's cry: *Caw, caw!* It means to "cry out *loudly* with an *urgent scream* or shriek, using . . . 'shouts that express *deep* emotion.'"[*] When Jesus cries out for us like this, what picture is John giving us of his heart?

---

[*] "2896. Krazó," Bible Hub, accessed February 12, 2025, https://biblehub.com/greek/2896.htm.

Drink Deep

"Whoever believes in me," Jesus says, "'out of his heart will flow rivers of living water'" (John 7:38, ESV).

- What do we need to do to receive this living water?
- What do you think it means to believe in Jesus?
- When Jesus says "out of his heart," this can refer, in the original language, to either *Jesus's* heart or *the believer's* heart. How do they work together like a faucet and sponge?

The Cross as Dynamite

"Up to that time the Spirit had not been given," John says, "since Jesus had not yet been glorified" (John 7:39).

- When is Jesus glorified in John's gospel?
- What ceremony did the priests do during the festival?
- How did this ceremony foreshadow the cross?
- Read John 19:34. How is the spear piercing Jesus's side like a dam breaking?
- What sacramental associations do blood and water have in John's gospel?

USE YOUR IMAGINATION

Contemplate this chapter's theme of divine dehydration. First, think of an area of your life where you're currently experiencing spiritual dryness. Perhaps it's a thought pattern you've been stuck in, a confusing situation you need wisdom for, or a painful area you desire to encounter Christ in. Imagine you're in a desert with that difficulty surrounding you; then read aloud Psalm 42:1–3:

> As the deer pants for streams of water,
>   so my soul pants for you, my God.
> My soul thirsts for God, for the living God.
>   When can I go and meet with God?
> My tears have been my food
>   day and night,
> while people say to me all day long,
>   "Where is your God?"

Pray, "Holy Spirit, I'm thirsty for you. What is the fear I'm living under or the lie the enemy is speaking? Please search my heart, search my circumstances, and reveal any deeper layers I may be unaware of. Reveal anything you wish me to know about the nature of this battle I'm facing." Listen for thirty seconds to a minute (or however long feels appropriate to you) and see if anything surfaces. (Don't feel pressure to force anything if nothing surfaces; the point is simply creating space to listen.)

Second, if God revealed something, hold it before him for this next movement. (If nothing surfaced, you can still walk through this movement.) Imagine Jesus on the cross, blowing the dam to bring the river of life flowing to you. Read aloud Psalm 42:7–8:

> Deep calls to deep
>   in the roar of your waterfalls;

all your waves and breakers
    have swept over me.

By day the LORD directs his love,
    at night his song is with me—
    a prayer to the God of my life.

Pray, "Jesus, what truth do you want to speak to me? I desire your wisdom. I'm thirsty for your presence and to grow closer to you through this. Please teach me to see from your perspective." Listen for thirty seconds to a minute (or however long feels appropriate to you).

Thank God for any clarity that surfaced. (*Reminder:* The Holy Spirit will never contradict God's Word, so weigh what you're sensing against Scripture. Also, the Holy Spirit is best discerned in Christlike community, so if anything confusing surfaced, talk to a trusted pastor or godly friend.)

Close by reading aloud Psalm 42:11:

Why, my soul, are you downcast?
    Why so disturbed within me?
Put your hope in God,
    for I will yet praise him,
    my Savior and my God.

REFLECT ON IT

1. This chapter opens with a time when I felt confused by an internal voice I couldn't discern the source of.

Was it God? The devil? Just my own head? Have you ever felt confused about the voice of God in your life? Or distant from his life-giving presence? What were the circumstances? How did you try to address it?

2. The Feast of Tabernacles celebrated God's provision of water for his people in the wilderness. What stood out to you from this chapter's discussion of this Old Testament backdrop to Jesus's invitation in John 7?

3. Jesus says he can give you "living water" (John 7:38), an ancient term for rivers and streams, which brought life to the surrounding land. In what areas of your life do you want to learn to rely more on the Holy Spirit—the life-giving presence of Jesus? What might it look like to have the river of God's presence flowing through your life? (*Hint:* Psalm 1 gives a great picture of this.)

4. Jesus cries out, "If anyone thirsts, let him come to me and drink" (John 7:37, ESV). Usually the thirsty cry out for water, but here the Living Water cries out for the thirsty. What does it do to your heart to hear of Jesus crying out for you—to know it's not about you going out to find God but about God coming to find you? What need do you want to bring to him today? (Pause to pray over someone if they bring up a significant need.)

5. Read the stories from Tom Brady and Billie Eilish on page 101. Why do you think success fails to fully satisfy? What is it we're actually longing for?

6. "Whoever believes in me," Jesus says, "'out of his heart will flow rivers of living water'" (John 7:38, ESV). Describe what you think it means to believe in Jesus.

How has this shown up in your own life? What practices or rhythms help you soak in Christ's Spirit, like a sponge under a faucet?

7. The cross is a dam-removal project. Consider this picture in relation to your life right now: What is the dam, what is the water, and what happens when the dam is removed? (For instance, you might say something like, "The cross of Jesus removes the dam of regret and shame, the water is him cleansing me, and I can now live in freedom and joy.")

8. Pray for one another, focusing on either an area of deep thirst (need) in your life right now or a way you'd like to grow in intimacy with and reliance on the Holy Spirit.

SESSION V

8

RAISE THE BAR

When You're Battling Guilt and Regret

What do you do when you're battling guilt and regret? Have you ever done things you wish you could take back? Hurt people you wish you could heal? Faced shame and rejection because of your actions? It can be easy to try to lower the bar. When your conscience is accusing you, it's easy to lawyer up and play your own defense attorney. Yet Jesus uses the opposite method to get you off the hook.

Jesus *raises* the bar. He raises the bar so high that we all find ourselves in need of mercy—a mercy he's more than ready to give. When you're battling guilt and regret, the God who is on your side can show you how to set your conscience free.

PREPARE YOUR HEART

Reflect on a time when you felt guilt or regret. What were the circumstances? How were others affected? Were you tempted to try to lower the bar to excuse your actions? Why do you think we're tempted to do this? How did you eventually experience resolution in the situation? How do you think God sees you at such times?

UNPACK IT

Movement 1: Where's Waldo?

The teachers of the law bring Jesus a woman caught in adultery: "In the Law Moses commanded us to stone such women. Now what do you say?" (John 8:5).

- This is a legal scene (the word *law* shows up multiple times). What role is Jesus positioned to play in this story?
- John says their question is "a trap" (verse 6). What danger does Jesus face if he says yes? What danger does he face if he says no?
- Faced with the question of Moses or mercy, what route does Jesus take?
- Read Leviticus 20:10. If the woman in John 8 was "caught in the act of adultery" (verse 4), who is missing from this scene?
- When Jesus doesn't condemn the woman caught in adultery, what double standard in the ancient world is he confronting?
- How does the Old Testament also confront this double standard? (*Hint:* See passages where powerful men were confronted after committing adultery, like King David in 2 Samuel 12 and the patriarch Judah in Genesis 38.)

Own Your Junk

The woman's executioners are focusing on what's wrong with her and ignoring what's wrong with themselves.

- Read Matthew 7:3–5. What principle are the woman's accusers violating?
- What difference can it make in the atmosphere of a conflict when someone follows Jesus's principle and starts by owning their own junk?

Movement 2: The First Stone

Jesus says, "Let any one of you who is without sin be the first to throw a stone at her" (John 8:7).

- Read Deuteronomy 17:7. Who was required to throw the first stone?
- Why would this requirement have helped curb a mob mentality?
- If the accusers were found to have lied or used entrapment, what punishment did they face?
- When Jesus says "any one of you who is without sin," what is he referring to instead of general sinlessness?

Movement 3: The Trial of Jealousy

Jesus "bent down and started to write on the ground with his finger" (John 8:6).

- Read Exodus 31:18. What legal document did Yahweh write with his finger?
- What Old Testament ritual from Numbers 5 do Jesus's actions here echo?

- How did this ritual echo the golden calf incident of Exodus 32?
- How did the ritual help a spouse suspected of adultery?

Conviction Versus Condemnation

Jesus brings conviction without condemnation. He says to the woman, "Neither do I condemn you; go, and from now on sin no more" (John 8:11, ESV).

- Which of Jesus's words here speak to conviction?
- Which of Jesus's words here speak to no condemnation?
- Why is Jesus the one person who could have legitimately condemned her?
- As this woman looks into Jesus's eyes, what expression do you think she sees?

Taking Our Place

John 8 opens with Jesus going up to the Mount of Olives at night, then into the temple courts at dawn.

- How does this foreshadow his crucifixion?
- How does the phrase "in the midst" in verse 3 foreshadow his crucifixion (NKJV)?
- Read Romans 8:1. Who no longer faces any condemnation?
- Read Galatians 3:13. How did Jesus break the curse of condemnation?

USE YOUR IMAGINATION

Reflect on a key moment from your life that's causing guilt or regret. While the trial of jealousy can seem archaic, it's actually loaded with powerful imagery. The woman of John 8 walks through the trial with Jesus as her high priest, and it sets her free. Let's walk through *your* trial—with that core memory you're wrestling with—so you can experience Jesus's freedom too.

1. *The suspect is brought before the priest at the temple.* Close your eyes and imagine yourself brought before Jesus in the temple courts. What do you feel in his presence with the memory exposed? Describe the memory to him by journaling it. Focus on your actions. Bring any guilt, regret, humiliation, fear, or other emotions to him in prayer.

2. *The priest sweeps dirt from the ground into an earthen cup filled with holy water and writes down the accusation against the suspect.* Journal what you're accused of. Focus on any condemnation you feel in your own conscience, as well as any hostility others may have toward you because of your actions.

3. *The accusation is then mixed into the holy water in the earthen vessel.* Jesus is the true temple—bearing the glorious presence of his divinity within the earthen vessel of his humanity—who brings us the living water of his Spirit. Imagine your accusation being swirled with the purity of his presence, drawing to the surface and exposing any truth he desires to convict you of. Journal any truth he's bringing to mind. (Take heart!

Remember that his goal is not to condemn you but to restore you to wholeness.)

4. *Next, a grain offering of barley was burnt on the altar.* Jesus is the Bread of Life. His miracle of turning barley bread into a meal for thousands (John 6) is a sign of his life given for his people on the cross. Imagine the bread of his body given for you. Journal your thanks for his sacrifice to make you his and to make you whole.

5. *Finally, the accused drinks the bitter water, and it surfaces their guilt or innocence.* Jesus drank your cup of condemnation so that you wouldn't have to. He bore your accusation on the cross to set you free. Journal your thanks for the freedom he's given. Pray about what it would look like for you to live more deeply into that freedom he gave his life for. In what areas do you need to trust his voice over the voice of the accuser and walk in that freedom?

With your eyes closed, imagine yourself standing before Jesus and hear him speak these words to you: "Neither do I condemn you; go, and from now on sin no more" (John 8:11, ESV).

REFLECT ON IT

1. *Raising the bar* is a metaphor for elevating the standard to make things harder. When you face guilt or regret, are you tempted to lower the bar to ease your conscience? If so, why do you think that is? Why is it counterintuitive for many of us to raise the bar in such

circumstances? What difference does it make knowing we have a savior?

2. Jesus confronts the double standard. The teachers of the law say the woman was "caught in the act of adultery" (John 8:4), but the guy is missing, though he's just as guilty. Have you ever felt crushed by the weight of a double standard? Felt the sting of a one-sided accusation from others when they were unwilling to apply the same level of critique to themselves? What was the experience like?

3. The accused woman is brought before Jesus with a mob ready to stone her. How do you imagine she felt? Have you ever been publicly exposed, embarrassed, or attacked? With humiliation, shame, fear, anger, or guilt coursing through your veins? What was the experience like?

4. Read Matthew 7:3–5. Why do you think we find faults in others more readily than we find them in ourselves? How can it change the atmosphere when you start by owning your junk?

5. Jesus says, "Let any one of you who is without sin be the first to throw a stone at her" (John 8:7). Why is the solution not *to minimize* others' sin but *to maximize* your awareness of your own sin? How does recognizing your own need for God's mercy change your posture toward those who have wronged you?

6. Jesus "bent down and started to write on the ground with his finger" (John 8:6). What stood out to you from this chapter's discussion of the trial of jealousy? If you did the Use Your Imagination exercise for this session, share any insights that emerged from it.

7. Jesus brings conviction without condemnation. He says, "Neither do I condemn you; go, and from now on sin no more" (John 8:11, ESV). What is Jesus's goal in confronting our sin? (*Hint:* Read John 3:17.) Why is it important that we fully own the reality of what we've done?

8. Jesus took our place at the cross. In Christ Jesus, there is no longer any condemnation for us (Romans 8:1). He broke the curse of condemnation by bearing our curse himself on that tree (Galatians 3:13). In what ways do you want to trust more deeply in the power of Christ's sacrifice for you? What would it look like for you to not only own your past sin but also "go, and from now on sin no more"—walking in the freedom Christ offers you?

9. Pray together, offering gratitude to Jesus for the freedom he's brought you and releasing to him any areas where you struggle with guilt, regret, or condemnation. Ask for the strength to sin no more as you live a life of worship and obedience in response to his great love. Consider closing by reading Romans 8:1–2.

9

OPEN YOUR EYES

When You Can't See Meaning or Purpose

Anton's syndrome is a condition where patients are blind but claim to be able to see. They bump into things and don't recognize faces but may explain it away, saying, "It seems dark in here"—unaware of the gravity of their condition.

While this is a rare physical condition, it's a common spiritual condition. In John 9, Jesus confronts those who are spiritually blind yet claim to be able to see. It's possible to stand before the Light of the World yet remain in the dark. It's possible to bump into God's redemptive work and think it's an obstacle, missing out on what he's doing right in front of you. Fortunately, however, Jesus is the Great Physician. He can open your eyes.

PREPARE YOUR HEART

When we face suffering, it can be easy to look backward and get fixated on trying to find a cause or person to blame—even if that person is yourself. This is understandable: We want to find meaning or purpose in our suffering. Jesus shows us a better way. But before we get there, reflect on an experience of suffering you have faced or are facing now. Were you tempted to look backward and get fixated on who or what was to blame? What explanations were you torn between? Did you wrestle with God during the experience? Was there resolution, or are you still in the middle of it? Pray and bring your heart before God as you prepare for this mini-session.

UNPACK IT

Looking Forward

Jesus's disciples ask, "Rabbi, who sinned, this man or his parents, that he was born blind?" Jesus responds, "Neither this man nor his parents sinned . . . but this happened so that the works of God might be displayed in him" (John 9:2–3).

- How do the disciples look backward to try to explain the man's condition?
- What were negative cultural beliefs at the time surrounding disabilities?
- How does Jesus look forward to address the man's condition?

Restoring the Image

Jesus uses an interesting method to open the man's eyes: "He spit on the ground, made some mud with the saliva, and put it on the man's eyes" (John 9:6).

- How do Jesus's actions toward the blind man reflect God's creation of Adam in Genesis 2?

- How is this a picture of Jesus restoring us as image-bearers?
- Jesus tells the man to "Go" and "wash in the Pool of Siloam" (John 9:7). What does John say the word *Siloam* means?
- How is this washing a picture of baptism?

Now I See

When the religious leaders interrogate the healed man, he simply responds, "One thing I do know. I was blind but now I see!" (John 9:25).

- What does this man model for how Jesus's followers can respond when their faith is opposed?
- Read Revelation 12:11. What two things does John say the saints overcame by?
- Read John 9:11. Who does the healed man make the hero of his story?
- How does the healed man model faith as "the assurance of things hoped for, the conviction of things not seen" (Hebrews 11:1, ESV)?

Healing as Judgment

Jesus confronts the religious leaders: "If you were blind, you would not be guilty of sin; but now that you claim you can see, your guilt remains" (John 9:41).

- How do these leaders have a spiritual version of Anton's syndrome (which causes a person to be unaware of their own blindness)?

- Read John 9:39. What kind of judgment has Jesus come to bring to the world?
- Read John 3:19–20. Why do some people not step into the light?

Light of the World

Jesus sees the blind man before the blind man ever sees Jesus. "Passing by," John 9 opens, "[Jesus] saw a man blind from birth" (verse 1, YLT).

- What is the phrase "passing by" associated with in the Old Testament?
- Read Exodus 33:21–23. What passed by Moses here?
- Read Job 9:11. How was Job like the blind man in John 9?
- The healing of the blind man is the sixth sign in John's gospel. How does it point to Jesus's death and resurrection?

USE YOUR IMAGINATION

Close your eyes. Imagine walking through an average day in your life in complete darkness, unable to see. Which activities would be difficult? Which would be impossible? Which would be unaffected? What work-arounds could you come up with to navigate your day?

Now imagine you've lived your entire life in that kind of darkness. Then one morning, you can see the sun rising. What emotions would you experience? What activities would you do first? Who would you tell first? How would you describe the impact?

Jesus, the Light of the World, has come to make this kind of difference in your life. The healed man tells his simple before-and-after story: "I was blind but now I see!" (John 9:25). How would you summarize the before and after of your story? What darkness or spiritual blindness did you experience before meeting Jesus? How did Jesus open your eyes to see the glory of God? What difference has Jesus made since you encountered him?

Who can you share this story with? Either a Christian you want to get to know better or a friend who is spiritually curious? (*Pro tip:* First ask your conversation partner about their story. Explain that you want to get to know them better; be genuinely interested in their thoughts, life, and experiences; and pray before you go to meet with them.)

REFLECT ON IT

1. Describe a time of suffering in your life when you looked backward to find a cause or person to blame. What was your situation? Was the culprit clear, or were there different possible explanations? Were you tempted to get fixated on the past? What was your experience with God like in this season? Share as much as you're comfortable with.
2. Read John 9:2–3. Why do you think Jesus calls us to look forward in hard times? What difference could it

make to ask how God's glory might be revealed through your difficult circumstances?

3. What struck you about this chapter's discussion of Jesus using mud to heal the man and how this echoes Genesis 2 and ancient ceremonies for making divine images? How does being an image-bearer, created to reflect God's glory in the world, change your everyday life?

4. Read John 9:25. The healed man's testimony is simple. When are you tempted to doubt the power of your testimony? How can you fall back on your story (of how Jesus has changed your life) when you face opposition to your faith?

5. Read John 9:8–9. The community can't believe this is the same man they knew before. Do people recognize a before and after in your story (that is, a difference Jesus has made in your life)? How would you summarize this before and after in a sentence or two? Describe the difference between making Jesus the hero of your story and making yourself the hero.

6. Jesus confronts the leaders: "If you were blind, you would not be guilty of sin; but now that you claim you can see, your guilt remains" (John 9:41). How is this like spiritual Anton's syndrome? Why do you think we have a hard time acknowledging our condition? What excuses have you been tempted to make to justify living apart from God? How might the practice of confession help you live in the light?

7. Jesus's healing of the blind man is the sixth sign of John's gospel. Describe how this miracle gives us a picture of the death and resurrection of Christ.

8. Jesus sees the blind man before the blind man ever sees Jesus. Similarly, the Great I Am sees you where you are, and the time is coming when you will see him too. While Jesus has opened your eyes spiritually, how can you trust him as you look forward to that day when you will see him face-to-face?

9. Close by praying for a person in your life whose eyes you desire to see opened to the glory of Jesus. Share enough with the group to pray together for that person, but avoid disclosing any confidential details about their life. If you are a large group, consider breaking into groups of two or three people to allow more time to pray for these specific people. Pray that Christ's light would overcome the darkness, their spiritual blindness would be healed, their hearts would be softened, and their eyes would be opened to the glory of Jesus.

SESSION VI

10

DISCOVER YOUR DEFENDER

When They Should Have Protected You but Didn't

Where do you go when they should have protected you but didn't? These experiences leave craters in your soul. It can be hard to trust again. Easy to feel like you're all alone. Natural to put up the defenses and not let anyone get too close. How do you avoid retreating into cynicism, suspicion, and isolation? Is there a way back to an abundant life?

In John 10, Jesus describes himself as the Good Shepherd. Whatever you've been through, he can bring you to greener pastures on the other side.

PREPARE YOUR HEART

Heads up: This chapter can enter into some sensitive subject matter. Is there a time when you were wounded by an authority figure? Perhaps a father, church leader, or boss? Jesus can meet you in your vulnerability, help you name the evil done to you, define the marks of good leadership, guide you through your valley of the shadow, and teach you to trust again. Take some time to prepare your heart in prayer. Ask the Good Shepherd to minister to you as you work through the questions ahead.

UNPACK IT

The Shepherd-King
The role of shepherd is a leadership image in the Bible.

- Why are kings and other leaders referred to as shepherds in the Bible?
- How does shepherding speak to the *purpose* of leadership? What qualities does it emphasize?
- How does Jesus embody the qualities of a good shepherd?

Thieves, Robbers, and Hired Hands
Jesus confronts three types of bad leaders in John 10. Describe each in their ancient context and identify the type of bad leader each might map onto today:

- thieves
- robbers
- hired hands

Jesus names what was done to you as evil. Knowing this is the first step toward healing. You have to be able to name what was done to you as wrong—even if only to yourself. If it's helpful, take some time to journal anything you sense Christ inviting you to name.

On Church Hurt

The word *pastor* means "shepherd." There's an important Old Testament backdrop to our good shepherd passage. In Ezekiel 34, God confronted Israel's leaders as bad shepherds who "only take care of yourselves" and don't "take care of the flock" (verse 2).

- Read Ezekiel 34:1–4. What were the bad shepherds doing?
- Read Ezekiel 34:5–6. What impact did this have on the sheep?
- Read Ezekiel 34:7–10. Why is it important that God named the shepherds' wrong?
- Read Ezekiel 34:11–16. What did God promise to come and do himself?

The Shepherd's Voice

Jesus guides his sheep. John 10:4–5 says, "He goes on ahead of them, and his sheep follow him because they know his voice. But they will never follow a stranger; in fact, they will run away from him because they do not recognize a stranger's voice."

- How is shepherding different between the Middle East and the Western Hemisphere?
- Why does this passage suggest it is important to distinguish Jesus's voice from the voices of strangers?

Open the Gate

The early church put the image of the Good Shepherd on their tombs.[*] They looked to the Good Shepherd to guide them through the valley of the shadow of death (literally) to green resurrection pastures.

- What are some parallels between Jesus's description of himself as the Good Shepherd (John 10) and his raising of Lazarus (John 11)?
- Why is the Good Shepherd a comfort for those facing death?

USE YOUR IMAGINATION

Jesus was hurt by the church. The central image of Christianity, the cross, is Christ being wounded by his people, mistreated by his leaders. While we're often tempted to use our wounds to distance ourselves from Christ, the reality is, properly understood, they can draw us closer to him.

Close your eyes and imagine Christ hanging on the cross. Envision the scourging on his body, the thorns piercing his head, the wound in his side. He meets you in your vulnerability. With this image in mind, bring the pain of your experience before him in prayer through the following four movements. Don't rush it; take as much time as you need in his presence.

---

[*] Kenneth E. Bailey, *The Good Shepherd: A Thousand-Year Journey from Psalm 23 to the New Testament* (IVP Academic, 2014), 21–22.

1. *Name the evil done to you.* Consider asking the Holy Spirit to walk you through the details of your experience, asking him to give you clarity on the nature of the injustice and the impact it's had on you.

2. *Bring that evil to the Lord.* Consider asking the Holy Spirit to meet you in your woundedness, ministering the presence of the crucified Christ, knowing that "by his wounds we are healed" as we encounter the balm of his presence in the brutality of our pain (Isaiah 53:5). (*Note:* This isn't to say prayer is a quick fix or substitute for other resources like counseling and community.)

3. *Seek the power to forgive.* Consider asking the Holy Spirit to release you from bitterness and set your heart free. (Remember, forgiveness doesn't mean you necessarily need to restore relationship with the person who wounded you, especially when there's a pattern of abuse; see page 156 on the difference between forgiveness and reconciliation.)

4. *If you're ready, pray for the person who wounded you.* When you can't find the strength within yourself to forgive, you can seek that strength by reflecting on how much you've been forgiven, by looking up to the Shepherd hanging on that cross, who declares "Father, forgive them" as he offers you his body and blood (Luke 23:34).

REFLECT ON IT

1. If you feel comfortable sharing, was there a time in your life when you were wounded by a leader who was supposed to care for you? Summarize the situation. Why do you think these kinds of wounds cut so deep?

2. In John 10, Jesus describes himself as the Good Shepherd. What stood out to you from this chapter's description of a shepherd as a leadership image? Did this challenge any associations you had with shepherding imagery from the Bible? How so?

3. Jesus names the evil actions of thieves, robbers, and hired hands. These speak, loosely, to deceptive treachery, violent coercion, and cowardly abandonment. Why is it important to name such evil? What are some reasons we struggle to name others' actions toward us as evil?

4. Read Ezekiel 34:1–10. What characterizes bad leadership in this passage? What indictment did God give bad leaders of his people? How seriously does God take such leadership? What impact does bad leadership have on the flock?

5. Read Ezekiel 34:11–16. What characteristics did God model here for leaders? How do these point to Christ as the Good Shepherd? Describe where you've experienced such leadership in the church.

6. Jesus goes ahead of his sheep to guide them. Why is this significant?

7. Since Jesus's sheep know his voice, "they will never follow a stranger" (John 10:5). How confident do you feel in your ability to distinguish Jesus's voice from the

voice of the enemy? What are some characteristics that distinguish these two voices? What role might Scripture, prayer, and healthy Christian community play in knowing the voice of your good shepherd?

8. Jesus calls Lazarus out of his grave, like a sheep from its pen. There are many parallels between Jesus's discussion of himself as the Good Shepherd (John 10) and his raising of Lazarus (John 11). Why did the early church put the image of the Good Shepherd on their tombs? How can looking to Christ as your good shepherd give you confidence and hope even in the face of the grave?

9. Close by having someone read Psalm 23 or reciting it together aloud.

11

WALK FREE

When Your Mind Is a Prison

Where do you go when you feel trapped in the prison of your own mind? When you assume God is the warden just waiting to drop the guillotine? If you had a pardon, why would you refuse it? What would it look like to walk free?

PREPARE YOUR HEART

Describe any messages you tend to hear on repeat in your own mind, any mistakes you've made that are hard to move on from, or any memories you tend to replay over and over. Bring those before God in prayer and ask him to prepare your heart to not only *know* you're forgiven but also *experience* his pardon.

UNPACK IT

The Great Exchange

Pilate finds nothing wrong with Jesus, but the people demand he release Barabbas instead. This section of *God Is on Your Side* highlights John's contrast of Jesus and Barabbas in the following three ways. What details stood out to you?

1. The innocent exchanged for the guilty
2. The King exchanged for a rebel
3. The beloved Son exchanged for an estranged son

To Set You Free

Barabbas is a picture of Israel and of us. Describe how each of these categories applied to Israel and how each applies to you:

1. Son of the Father
2. Rebel
3. Guilty

In Our Place

Many people struggle with the idea of substitution, an innocent person being exchanged for the guilty.

- How is Jesus an active agent, not a passive victim, as he goes to the cross?
- Where does Jesus say Pilate's authority comes from?
- Read John 10:18. Beyond his substitution on the cross, what authority does Jesus also have that is greater than the grave?

Confronting Two Lies

It's astounding that George Wilson said no to President Jackson's pardon. Yet many people say no to Jesus's even greater pardon.

- How is Jesus's pardon, offered in the gospel, even greater than that offered to George Wilson?
- What is the first lie that can lead us to reject Jesus's pardon?
- What is the second lie that can lead us to reject Jesus's pardon?
- Which lie are you more tempted by?

USE YOUR IMAGINATION

Imagine Barabbas's last night on death row. Try to understand his experience. While this exercise is speculative, the deeper goal is to reflect on the human condition, which Barabbas represents. With that in mind, journal your answers to the following questions:

- What emotions do you imagine Barabbas was experiencing? For any emotion you list, why was he experiencing that particular one?
- What memories were replaying in his head? Were they negative memories marked by regret or positive memories marked by longing?
- What thoughts did he have about his family and friends?
- What were his prayers that night to God?

Now imagine Barabbas's experience when he heard the news of his pardon.

- What emotions do you imagine Barabbas was experiencing now? What was it like to see that prison door swing open?
- Describe the scenes you imagine when he walked out of the prison into the sunlight, into the city, and when he saw his family and friends. What was the content of their first conversation?
- Write out a prayer to God, putting yourself in Barabbas's shoes, with the words you would want to pray, having experienced that newfound freedom.

REFLECT ON IT

1. Recap the story of George Wilson refusing the presidential pardon. Why do you think he rejected the pardon? How is this a parable for refusing the gospel?
2. Do you ever get stuck in your head? To the extent you feel comfortable sharing, summarize the messages, memories, or mistakes that are hard to move on from.
3. Read John 18:38–40. Which of these three contrasts stands out most to you, and why?
   a. The innocent exchanged for the guilty
   b. The King exchanged for a rebel
   c. The beloved Son exchanged for an estranged son
4. Substitution is a powerful theme in movies and literature. Read the movie montage on page 164. Which of these movie moments most captivated your heart

when you first saw it? What other scenes of substitution in movies or books have gripped you? Why do you think these blockbuster images captivate our hearts? Why is this substitution theme so powerful and enduring?

5. What do you think Barabbas's last night on death row was like? Describe what you imagine his experience was like before his pardon and then after he received news of it and walked free. How is this a picture of our life under both the power of sin and the freedom Christ came to bring?

6. When it comes to the gospel, one reason people reject God's pardon is they believe *I'm not that bad.* Describe this lie and why the gospel says it's inaccurate. Include any ways you struggle with it or have seen it hold back other people you know (without identifying them by name).

7. A second reason people reject the pardon is they believe *I'm too bad.* Describe this lie and why the gospel says it's inaccurate. Include any ways you struggle with it or have seen it hold back other people you know (without identifying them by name).

8. Close in prayer. Consider using one of the following methods: (a) If one person in the group is really struggling with walking into freedom in a particular area, have everyone lay hands on this person (if they're comfortable with that) and pray for them. Or (b) break into groups of two or three people and pray for one another to live more deeply into freedom in particular areas.

SESSION VII

12

ANTICIPATE SURPRISE

When It Hurts to Hope

Where do you go when it hurts to hope? When God's gone missing and you're left to fend for yourself? Where do you go when the rug gets pulled out from under you and you feel like you have no future? It may sound counterintuitive, but the gospel invites you to the hard place. The place of the wound. Go to the tomb.

PREPARE YOUR HEART

Is there a painful area of loss in your life that you've had trouble revisiting? Bring that before the Holy Spirit and ask him to prepare your heart for this mini-session. Consider sharing any fear or trepidation you have that makes it difficult to revisit this wound. Remember that he is gentle, patient, and kind. As you pray, jot down any reflections that come to mind before you begin.

UNPACK IT

Your Darkest Hour

Mary Magdalene's encounter with the resurrected Jesus occurs "early on the first day of the week" (John 20:1).

- In the prior week, what day did Jesus enter Jerusalem? What day was he crucified? What day did he rest in the grave?
- What is the significance of his resurrection occurring on a new first day?
- What other new-creation motifs show up in this scene?

A Sign of Love

When Mary arrives at the tomb, John highlights details that echo powerful themes.

- Mary weeps at the tomb (John 20:11). Earlier in John's gospel, Jesus wept at Lazarus's tomb (John 11:35). How can tears be a sign of love?
- Mary looks into the empty tomb and sees two angels sitting on the slab where Jesus slept: "one at the head and the other at the foot" (verse 12). How does this echo the ark of the covenant in the Old Testament?
- What did the sprinkling of blood on the ark accomplish in the Old Testament? How is this related to Christ's death and what it accomplished?

Who Is It You Seek?

Jesus asks Mary, "Who is it you seek?" (John 20:15, my translation).

- When was the other time Jesus asked this question, and who was he speaking to?
- Who does Mary represent here?
- Before Mary met Jesus, how was her life like Jesus's tomb?

Jesus asks Mary, "Woman, why are you crying?" (John 20:15). That term "woman" shows up in four crucial scenes earlier in John's gospel. Write down who Jesus is speaking to in each passage; then in a single sentence explain how each interaction points to what Christ has come to accomplish.

- "Woman . . . my hour has not yet come" (John 2:4).
- "Woman . . . a time is coming and has now come when the true worshipers will worship the Father in the Spirit and in truth" (John 4:21, 23).
- "Woman . . . neither do I condemn you; go, and from now on sin no more." (John 8:10–11, ESV).
- "Woman, behold, your son!" (John 19:26, ESV).

Hold On

At first, Mary thinks Jesus is the gardener.

- When does Mary recognize the person she's speaking to is Jesus?

- Jesus says, "Do not hold on to me" (John 20:17). What associations does that term "hold on to" have in the Bible?
- "Do not hold on to me" can sound cold. Why does Jesus say this?

USE YOUR IMAGINATION

The entrance to Israel's temple faced east, toward the rising sun. Imagine sitting at the gate of the temple before dawn and setting your gaze eastward. What kinds of prayers do you pray in that deepest dark?

While contemplating this image, name any areas of darkness you're currently experiencing (or past areas you've avoided dealing with). Bring them before the Lord in prayer, asking the Holy Spirit to guide you and give you the courage to face them. Then write down anything that stands out from your time in prayer.

"It's always darkest before the dawn," my grandpa used to say. The gospel affirms this. Imagine the sun now beginning to rise on the temple as you sit at its gate.

While contemplating this image, imagine what it would look like for the light of God's presence to surprise you in these areas of your life. Bring your longing and hope for such renewal to the Lord. Ask him to shine on your heart with the glory of his presence. Ask him to transform and heal your circumstances. Ask for his hope to sustain you in any areas that must wait for renewal until the resurrection.

REFLECT ON IT

1. Mary goes to the tomb. Have you ever lost someone or something that was precious to you? How did you cope, whether through prayer, counseling, or journaling? Why is it worth having the guts to face such losses and process them with God and others (versus running from the pain)?

2. Mary cries at the tomb of Jesus. Why do you think our culture is often uncomfortable with grief? How can tears be a sign of love? When have your tears been a sign of your love for someone or something you lost?

3. The angels sat on the slab where Christ had lain, like the angels on the ark of the covenant in the Old Testament, "one at the head and the other at the foot" (John 20:12). What is it about Jesus's presence that is able to turn our hard places into holy places? When have you experienced his transforming presence in an area of great loss?

4. Jesus asks, "Who is it you seek?" (John 18:4; 20:15, my translation). He asks both Mary (who wants to worship him) and the soldiers (who want to crucify him). Why do you think our motives matter when it comes to seeking Jesus? Describe some different motives people can have for attending church, exploring spirituality, or dabbling with religion. Which are good, and which are not? What motives do you want to have for seeking Jesus?

5. Jesus calls Mary "Woman." That term—as it's used in John's gospel—sets her up as a representative for the church. What stands out to you from this chapter

about Mary as a picture of the church? Which of these themes that she exemplifies do you see at work in your own life currently, and which do you want to grow in?

6. Jesus tells Mary not to hold on to him. That can sound cold, but what reason does this chapter give for him saying this (see page 184)? In what way is Jesus present with us as the church today, and in what way are we still waiting to "hold on to him" in the coming kingdom? How can this hope provide comfort for us today?

7. Jesus tells Mary *his* Father has become *our* Father. How do Jesus's death and resurrection make us a new family? What do you think it means for us to treat one another in the church like family? When have you experienced the church as family in a tangible way?

8. Jesus's resurrection changes everything. Take time to pray for one another, that each of you would "go to the tomb" to face difficult parts of your past and "anticipate surprise" from the resurrection power of God today.

13

CHANGE THE WORLD

When Your Past Seems Bigger than Your Future

Do you have memories that haunt you? You can wrestle with God. *Am I being punished or persecuted? Facing the consequences of wrong I've done or enduring the wickedness of others? Jesus, have you left the building? Where are you in the midst of it all? Do you see me? If so, how do you see me?*

Where do you go when your past seems bigger than your future?

PREPARE YOUR HEART

Ask Jesus to tenderly walk you back into any memories of regret you want to process—not to shame you, but to restore you. Pray for the Holy Spirit to prepare your heart, to transform your regret, and to call you into a better future.

UNPACK IT

Gather the Nations

Jesus approaches Peter and the other disciples after they've fished all night and caught nothing.

- What are two clues in John 21:2–3 that Peter is still a leader?
- What are a few parallels between this scene and the moment Jesus first called Peter (Luke 5:1–11)?
- How is the miraculous catch of fish a sign of Peter's call to gather the nations?
- What is the significance of catching 153 fish? How about the nets not being torn (when compared with Luke 5:6–7)?

Breakfast on the Beach

Jesus cooks breakfast on the beach for the disciples.

- Jesus cooks over a charcoal fire. What scene does the charcoal fire echo from earlier in John's gospel?
- Jesus asks three times, "Do you love me?" (John 21:15–17). What question was Peter asked three times earlier in John's gospel?
- How did Peter respond to the earlier question, and how does he respond here?
- Based on your answers above, why does Jesus set up this scene and ask Peter this question? How does this story reveal the heart of God?

Stinky Clothes

Jesus tells Peter to "feed my sheep" (John 21:17).

- How do the images of a shepherd and a fisherman each speak to a distinct aspect of Peter's calling?
- What does the word *pastor* mean?
- What does this passage suggest are the marks of a good pastor?
- How does this calling apply more broadly to all of us who follow Jesus?

Give Your Life

Jesus foreshadows Peter's future.

- What is meant by Peter stretching out his hands and someone else dressing him and leading him somewhere he doesn't want to go?
- Why do you think Jesus tells Peter this? Is the reason to scare him, to give him courage, or something else?

Water to Wine

Jesus doesn't call Peter to do something he hasn't first done himself.

- How does Jesus fish for Peter in this scene?
- How does Jesus feed Peter as his lamb in this scene?
- How did Jesus give his life for Peter before he calls Peter to give his life in response?

USE YOUR IMAGINATION

Jesus uses three powerful images here for Peter's calling. Each speaks to a different aspect of following Jesus. Take time to contemplate each of these images:

1. *Fisherman.* Close your eyes and imagine yourself as a fisherman or fisherwoman. What kind of preparation is involved in getting the boat, nets, and crew ready? What kind of patience is involved in waiting for the right time? What kind of longing is involved in hoping for a great catch? What kind of conditions are endured in storms? What is it like to experience a large catch?

   How does this deepen your desire to gather people to Jesus?

2. *Shepherd.* Close your eyes and imagine yourself as a sheep. What is it like when you're hungry and unsure where to find food? When you're lost and don't know how to get home? When you're wounded by a predator and unable to clean or bandage the wound? What is it like when the shepherd arrives to carry, feed, bandage, and heal you?

   How does this deepen your desire to care for Jesus's people?

3. *Martyr.* Close your eyes and imagine waiting for your execution as a martyr for your faith. What do you feel in your gut that morning as you anticipate what's coming? What is it like as someone undresses you for the humiliation of dying naked before the crowds? As they

lead you in chains or at spearpoint somewhere you
don't want to go? As they stretch out your hands to
embrace the fate the Father has allowed you to endure for the glory of his Son? What kind of intimacy
do you feel with Jesus, who gave his life for you?

How does this deepen your desire to give your life
for Jesus?

REFLECT ON IT

1. Are there memories that haunt you? Mistakes you've
   made that you're unsure Christ could really forgive
   you for? Areas where your past seems bigger than
   your future? Summarize this to the extent you feel
   comfortable.

2. Why do you think Peter goes back to fishing, even
   though he knows Jesus is alive? Where do you tend to
   go when your memories of failure make it difficult to
   believe God could want to use you? John 21:2–3 still
   depicts Peter as a leader, even though he's not yet
   walking in his calling. What natural strengths or gifts
   has God given you?

3. The miraculous catch is a sign of Peter's calling to
   gather the nations. Does sharing your faith scare you
   or excite you? What negative associations with evangelism have caused you to shy away from it? How might
   a vision of God's renewal in your city or town motivate
   a healthy version of sharing your faith?

4. Jesus cooks over a charcoal fire and asks Peter three
   times, "Do you love me?" (John 21:15–17), intention-

ally echoing Peter's denial of him. Why do you think Jesus would intentionally surface our painful memories of mistakes or regrets? What are the dangers of ignoring these parts of our stories? How much do you struggle to trust Jesus with guiding you into painful memories? When has he done this in your life?

5. Jesus asks Peter to feed and care for his sheep. What do you think it means for the church to feed God's people? What about to care for God's people? The word *pastor* means "shepherd." When have you experienced good examples of church leaders who have done this in your life? Bad examples who haven't? More broadly, how might Jesus be calling you to feed and care for his people?

6. Jesus tells Peter the kind of death he will die: as a martyr for the gospel. Why do you think Jesus sometimes calls us to do difficult things? Where can we find courage to do them? What difficult thing might Jesus be calling you to do in this season of life?

7. Jesus doesn't call Peter to do anything he hasn't first done himself. How has Jesus fished for you? How has he fed and cared for you? How has he given his life for you? Why is it significant that we first receive from Jesus before we try to do things for Jesus?

8. Close your time together in prayer, with each person choosing one of the following three themes, then praying out loud:

   a. *Fisherman.* Pray for a specific person who doesn't know God, whom you sense God might be calling you to share your faith with.

b. *Shepherd.* Pray for a person in the church who is going through a difficult time, whom you sense God might be calling you to care for.

c. *Martyr.* Pray about something difficult you sense God might be calling you to do, for clarity, wisdom, and courage to do the right thing.

CONCLUSION

Be the Beloved

What do you want on your tombstone? What do you want your legacy to be? Perhaps an accomplishment or trophy? A passion or hobby? The apostle John concludes his gospel by identifying himself as "the disciple whom Jesus loved" (John 21:20). That's how he wants to be remembered. That's the legacy he puts on his tombstone. That's his way of saying there's no greater identity, no deeper calling he desires, than to be the beloved of God.

This is how you live in response to the God who is on your side: You be the beloved.

PREPARE YOUR HEART

As we put a bow on this book, what major themes have had the most impact on you thus far? Jot them down.

UNPACK IT

A Beloved Disciple
Beloved is a theme in the Bible. How does each of these points speak to an identity as the beloved of God?

- King David's name
- Israel personified as the woman in Song of Songs
- Jesus's baptism

Intimacy with Jesus
John closes his gospel by describing himself as "the one who had leaned back against Jesus at the supper" (John 21:20).

- At the Last Supper, John is "in Jesus's bosom" (John 13:23, ASV). How is this location a picture of intimacy, security, and vulnerability?
- John 1:18 says the Son is "in the bosom of the Father" (NKJV). How does this verse help us understand the significance of John 13:23?

On Your Side
John could've written about many other things that Jesus did, he says, "but these are written that you may believe that Jesus is the Messiah, the Son of God, and that by believing you may have life in his name" (John 20:31).

- Why did John write his gospel?
- How does knowing this purpose help explain which one-on-one encounters and "I am" statement stories John chose to include in his gospel?

- What effect does John hope this will have in the life of the reader?
- How does John's purpose statement relate to this book's theme: that you could know—not just know *about*, but know *personally*—the God who is on your side?

USE YOUR IMAGINATION

Imagine it's your funeral. Write a eulogy that represents what you hope people would say about you. Consider which of its elements are résumé virtues and which are eulogy virtues (see page 203). After you finish writing this eulogy, ask Jesus to make you this kind of person with the years you have left—not as a way to earn God's love, but rather as a response to God's love. Ask the Holy Spirit to help you *be* the beloved.

REFLECT ON IT

1. Why do you think John refers to himself as "the disciple whom Jesus loved" (John 21:20), rather than using his name? What do you want on your tombstone, so to speak? In other words, how do you want to be remembered?

2. Recap the difference between résumé virtues and eulogy virtues. How would you describe the ideal relationship between them? What virtues of each category most stand out to you? What eulogy virtues do you most hope to grow in?

3. What role do you think intimacy, security, and vulnerability play in your relationship with God? How do

you want to grow in these areas in the season ahead? What practical steps do you feel led to take in this direction?

4. What is the difference between *creating* an identity and *receiving* an identity? How can the former create pressure and the latter create freedom? How have you experienced this pressure, or how do you want to grow in experiencing this freedom?

5. What role do the Word and Spirit play in receiving the love of God? How can you approach practices of spiritual formation not as rituals for *performing* but rather as postures for *receiving*?

6. How does starting with God's love for you keep you from legalism? How does it keep you from lawlessness? Which of these two do you tend to struggle with?

7. You are loved by the One who has no tombstone. How can you live more deeply into your identity as God's beloved? What rhythms or practices do you want to carry into the season ahead to root your life in his love?

8. What major themes have had the most impact on you during the journey through this book? Close in prayer together, thanking Christ for these themes and for being the God who is on your side.

JOSHUA RYAN BUTLER is a teaching pastor with the Willamette family of churches in the Portland area and the author of *The Party Crasher, Beautiful Union, The Skeletons in God's Closet,* and *The Pursuing God.* Josh loves shifting paradigms to help people who wrestle with tough topics of the Christian faith by confronting popular caricatures and replacing them with the beauty and power of the real thing. He and his wife, Holly, along with their three children, live in Portland. They enjoy spending time with friends over great meals and exploring the scenic beauty of the Pacific Northwest.

ABOUT THE TYPE

This book was set in Caledonia, a typeface designed in 1939 by W. A. Dwiggins (1880–1956) for the Merganthaler Linotype Company. Its name is the ancient Roman term for Scotland, because the face was intended to have a Scottish-Roman flavor. Caledonia is considered to be a well-proportioned, businesslike face with little contrast between its thick and thin lines.

DISCOVER THE LIFE-TRANSFORMING TRUTH THAT GOD IS FOR YOU.

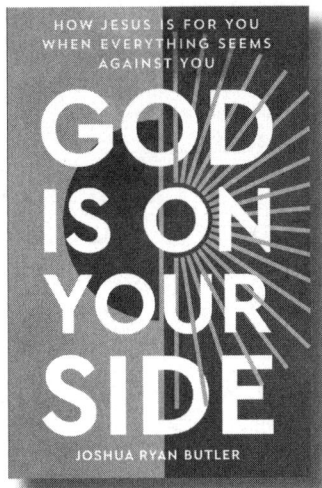

This book is for those haunted by a nagging sense that God is indifferent or disappointed in them. Learn that our greatest comfort is not what we've done to win God's love, but all God's love has done to win us.

This practical, illuminating, author-curated companion guide to *God Is on Your Side* encourages exploration of the goodness of God in a confusing world.

Also from author and pastor
JOSHUA RYAN BUTLER

In this insightful, nonpartisan road map toward faithful political engagement and ultimate allegiance to Jesus, pastor Joshua Ryan Butler diagnoses the roots of political conflict tearing apart the church and prescribes a practical and prophetic way forward.

Learn more about Joshua Ryan Butler's books at waterbrookmultnomah.com.

01 14